Mr. Jacobs: A Tale of the Drummer the Reporter and the Prestidigitateur

Arlo Bates

ESPRIOS DIGITAL PUBLISHING

MR. JACOBS

A TALE
OF
THE DRUMMER THE REPORTER
AND THE PRESTIDIGITATEUR

SEVENTH EDITION

BOSTON
W. B. CLARKE & CARRUTH
1883

CHAPTER I.

In spite of Jean-Jacques and his school, men are not everywhere, especially in countries where excessive liberty or excessive tiffin favors the growth of that class of adventurers most usually designated as drummers, or by a still more potent servility, the ruthless predatory instinct of certain bold and unscrupulous persons may and almost certainly will; and in those more numerous and certainly more happy countries where the travelling show is discouraged, the unwearying flatterer, patient under abstemious high-feeding, will assuredly become a roving sleight-of-hand man.

Without doubt the Eastern portion of the world, when an hereditary, or, at least, a traditional, if not customary, or, perhaps, conservative, not to say legendary, or, more correctly speaking, historic, despotism has never ceased to ingrain the blood of Russia, Chinese, Ottoman, Persia, India, British, or Nantasket, in a perfect instance of a ruthless military tiffin, where neither blood nor stratagem have been spared.[1]

[1]The editor was here obliged to omit a score of pages, in which the only thing worth preserving was a carcanet of sulphur springs.

I was at tiffin. A man sat opposite whose servant brought him water in a large goblet cut from a single emerald. I observed him closely. A water-drinker is always a phenomenon to me; but a water-drinker who did the thing so artistically, and could swallow the fluid without wincing, was such a manifestation as I had never seen.

I contrasted him with our neighbors at the lunch-counter, who seemed to be vying, like the captives of Circe, to ascertain by trial who could swallow the most free lunch, and pay for the fewest "pegs,"—those vile concoctions of spirits, ice, and soda-water, which have destroyed so many splendid resolutions on the part of the Temperance Alliance,—and an impression came over me that he must be the most innocent man on the road.

Before I go farther let me try and describe him. His peculiarity was that, instead of eyes, he had jewels composed of six precious stones. There was a depth of life and vital light in them that told of the pent-up force of a hundred, or, at least, of ninety-nine generations of Persian magi. They blazed with the splendor of a god-like nature, needing neither tiffin nor brandy and soda to feed their power.

My mind was made up. I addressed him in Gaelic. To my surprise, and somewhat to my confusion, he answered in two words of modern Hebrew. We fell into a polyglot but refined conversation.

"Come and smoke," he said, at length.

Slipping into the office of the hotel, and ascertaining that there was no danger, I followed to his room.

"I am known as Mr. Jacobs," he said. "My lawful name is Abdallah Hafiz-ben-butler-Jacobi."

The apartment, I soon saw, was small,—for India at least,—and every available space, nook, and cranny, were filled with innumerable show-cases of Attleboro' jewelry.

Mr. Jacobs

"Pretty showy?" he remarked familiarly. "I am a drummer."

"My name is Peter Briggs," I replied. "I am a correspondent of the *Calcutta Jackal*."

"My star!" he said. "That is the dog-star. A sudden thought strikes me," he added. "Let us swear an eternal friendship."

He thereupon told me his entire history, from childhood up. It was interesting to the last degree, as I had thought often before, when I read it in various dime novels.

He ceased speaking, and the waning moon rose pathetically, with a curiously doleful look, expressive of quiet, but deep contempt.

CHAPTER II.

The next morning I had tiffin.

I speculated in regard to Mr. Jacobs. A long and eventful experience with three-card monte men had made me extremely shy of persons who begin an acquaintance by making confidences; and I wondered why he had taken the trouble to make up the story of his life, to relate to an entire stranger. Still, there was something about the man that seemed to promise an item for the *Calcutta Jackal*, and therefore, when Jacobs appeared, looking like the sunflower, for all his wild dress and his knee-breeches, I felt the "little thrill of pleasure," so aptly compared by Swinburne to the clutch of a hand in the hair.

"Are you married?" queried Mr. Jacobs.

"Thank heavens, no!" I replied, convulsively. "Are you?"

"Some," returned he, gloomily. "I have three. They do not agree. Do you think a fourth wife would calm them?"

"A man," I observed, sententiously, "is better off with no wife at all than with three."

His subtle mind caught the flaw instantly.

"Negative happiness," he murmured; "very negative. Oh, I would I could marry all the sweet creatures!"

Having our tiffins saddled, we rode off at a breakneck pace, and cleverly managed to ride down the uncle of the heroine.

Mr. Jacobs

"Dear uncle," casually remarked that young lady, riding up, "I hope you are not hurt."

"What an original remark!" exclaimed Jacobs, with rapture. "Miss Eastinhoe is beautiful and sensible. I like her. What do you suppose she is worth?"

CHAPTER III.

Having tiffined, we reclined upon a divan.

"My father," said Mr. Jacobs, "had but one wife; I have already raised him two, as I told you, and mean to go him one better."

I smoked in silence.

"A hint for the *Calcutta Jackal*," I thought, with satisfaction. "Bigamy raised to the third power."

"You are right," he said, slowly, his half-closed eyes fixed on his feet; "yes, you are right. But why not?"

I shook myself, drank some sherbert, and kicked off one shoe impatiently. This reading of a gentleman's private thoughts seemed to me an unwarrantable impertinence; but a sudden light flashed over my obscured intellect, and, observing that he was in a trance, I felt it would be indelicate to argue the matter. I fired my shoe at him, to assure myself of his condition, and then held a free pass towards him. He instantly recovered, and stretched out his hand to take it.

"I must have been dreaming," he said, a look of annoyance shading his features as I drew the pass away. "But I am in love."

It was near midnight, and the ever-decreasing moon was dragging herself up, as if ashamed of her waning beauty and tearful look.

CHAPTER IV.

We called upon Miss Eastinhoe the following day. She was playing with a half-tamed young tiffin, a charming little beast, with long gray fur and bright twinkling eye, mischievous and merry as a gnome's. He was a gift of Mr. Jacobs to the lady. He cost nothing.

"Are you spoken for?" Miss Eastinhoe asked, her eyes opening a moment and meeting his, but falling again instantly with a change of color.[2]

[2]The editor had his doubts about this; but as it so stands in the original MS. (p. 69), concludes that in low latitudes, eyes do change color on slight provocation.

"Miss Eastinhoe," he said, quietly, "you know I am a man of muscle, and that I have three wives."

"Oh, I had forgotten!" she said; "I forgot about your wives."

"Among primitive people, and persons in pinafores," I interposed, "marriage is a social law."

"You surprise me, Mr. Briggs," she said, with an air of childlike simplicity.

I felt that I had put a plug into my end of the conversation.

"We will play polo next week," said Mr. Jacobs. "Meanwhile, let us visit a Certain Mighty Personage."

CHAPTER V.

"We will go at four," said Jacobs, coming into my room after tiffin. "I said three this morning, but it is not a bad plan to keep natives waiting."

"Why do we go?" I inquired, languidly.

"The Certain Mighty Personage has a prisoner whom I wish to purchase."

"Who is it?"

Leaning over until his mouth almost touched my ear, he whispered quietly:

"Number One."

"The devil, you say!" I ejaculated, surprised out of grammar and decorum by the startling news.

"Are you thinking of marrying Miss Eastinhoe?" I demanded, after a pause of some tiffins.

"Yes," he answered, "if her settlements are satisfactory."

Arrived at the residence of the Certain Mighty Personage, we were received in a jemadar where a sahib charpoyed the sowans and tiffined the maharajah.

"I'll have you exposed in the newspapers," said Jacobs, sternly, to the Certain Mighty Personage, "if you do not deliver into my hands, before the dark half of the next moon, the man Number One."

Mr. Jacobs

The Uncertain Mighty Personage signed a contract to that effect, with extreme reluctance, and with many forcible remarks disrespectful to both the ancestors and posterity of Jacobs.

"What do you want of Number One?" I inquired, as we rode away.

"He is the only man alive that can keep a plated watch from turning black in this accursed climate."

"But why did you bring me along, when you didn't need me?"

"To frighten him with the threat of the *Calcutta Jackal*. Besides, how else could you tell the story?"

CHAPTER VI.

We rode our tiffins back and met Miss Eastinhoe with her friends.

"Let us go on a tiger-hunt," we all remarked, casually.

As we drove home a voice suddenly broke on the darkness.[3]

[3] Another curious Oriental phenomenon, not sufficiently explained by the author.

"Peace, Abdallah Hafiz," it said.

"By the holy poker, the Jibena-inosay!" answered Jacobs, who had recognized the broken voice.

"I have business with thee," continued the voice; "I will be with thee, anon."

"It is Lamb Ral," my companion explained, as the voice faded away. "Facetious as ever; now you have him, and then again you don't have him. We call him the Little Joker, for short."

"Isn't he difficult to explain?" I ventured.

"Very," he said. "But who has ever explained how a man could keep his family up for years with no visible means of support; or how a person can promenade on his ear; or crawl into a hole and pull the hole in after him. And yet you have seen those things, I have seen them, everybody has seen them, and most of us have done them ourselves."

Later in the evening we were visited by Lamb Ral.

Mr. Jacobs

"Do not go tiger-hunting," he said. "It will take you out of the lines of the jewellery trade."

"Still I shall go," persisted Jacobs.

"What a singular piece of workmanship is that ytaghan!" observed Lamb Ral, waving one delicate hand towards the wall behind us.

When we turned back from seeing that there was no ytaghan there, the magician had disappeared, leaving a strong smell of lucifer matches behind him, but taking a number of triple-plated watches.

"Singular man," said Jacobs, musingly. "I wish I knew how he does it. It must be profitable."

CHAPTER VII.

We had tiffin with Miss Eastinhoe. Mr. Jacobs, in evening dress, looked surpassingly lovely.

CHAPTER VIII.

In the third game of polo a clumsy player struck Mr. Jacobs on the back of his head, laying open his skull. The wounded man fell from his saddle, but his foot caught in the stirrup, and he was dragged several miles by the infuriated Arab pony.

"Don't give him brandy," remarked Miss Eastinhoe, calmly. "Water will do quite as well. It is cheaper, and, as he is insensible, he will not know the difference."

"Thank you," replied Jacobs, gracefully tying his head together with a white woollen shawl. "We will start on the tiger hunt to-morrow."

He carefully lighted a cigarette and rode home.

"Briggs," Jacobs said, producing a mysterious trick bottle, "do as I tell you or you are a dead man. Stuff this wax into your nose, and bathe the back of my neck with this powerful remedy unknown to your Western medicine. I shall then fall asleep. If I do not wake before midnight, I shall sleep until breakfast time. You can easily arouse me by pressing the little silver knob behind my left ear. If you cannot remember, write it down."

Being a newspaper man, I naturally took out an old letter upon which to jot down his instructions. I faithfully carried out all his directions, and it is to be remarked in passing that on removing the wax from my nostrils, I was conscious of a strong odor of Scotch whiskey.

CHAPTER IX.

We started on our tiger-hunt. Miss Eastinhoe rode on an elephant, about which Jacobs, who loved the saddle, circled gayly, keeping up a fire of little compliments and pretty speeches of which he had thoughtfully brought a tiffinful with him, but to which the lady very fortunately soon became inured. He had also taken the precaution to have relay's of runners bring fresh roses half-way across India every morning for Miss Eastinhoe, whom he amused meantime by playing beautifully on the tiffin and warbling Persian love-songs.

CHAPTER X.

Guided only by a native tiffin, upon whom he showered an astonishing profusion of opprobrious epithets, Mr. Jacobs went forth in the dark and stilly night, and slaughtered a huge man-eating tiger, for whose ears Miss Eastinhoe had expressed a singular, but well-defined longing. The beast measured twenty-four feet, and, by stretching the story a little, I was able to say twenty-seven.

"My dear fellow," I said, "I am sincerely glad to see you back alive."

"Thank you, old man," he said, falling easily into English slang. "Do you know I have a superstition that I must fulfil every wish of hers. Besides, the skin will fetch a capital price."

"I adore you," murmured Miss Eastinhoe. "I shall have the ears pickled."

CHAPTER XI.

An old yogi stood near an older well. He put a stone in the bucket, and the slave could not draw it up. Suddenly the bottom came out, and the stout water-carrier fell headlong backwards on the grass.

"Did you ever see anything of that kind before, Miss Eastinhoe?" I inquired.

"No, indeed," she replied. "I always before supposed that to fall headlong a man must go forwards."

"I am off to see a Certain Mighty Personage," Mr. Jacobs remarked, stooping casually from his saddle to kiss Miss Eastinhoe on her white gold hair, which shone so that it made the moon look, on the whole, rather sickly, as an electric light pales the gas-jet. "If I want you, I'll send for you. Lamb Ral has a Star Route contract and will bring you word."

He rode away, and I pensively smoked my tiffin.

CHAPTER XII.

The afternoon mail brought me a postal-card:

"I shall want you after all. Please ride night and day for a week. It is a matter of life and death."

Changing horses every five or six miles, I rode over the greater part of Asia, subsisting on a light but elegant diet of chocolate caramels. Then I stopped to take tiffin with a striking-looking fellow in a dirty brown cloth *caftan* Jacobs' face changed when I gave him a silver box Miss Eastinhoe sent him.

"I gave her this myself;" he said; "it is only plated."

"Mr. Briggs," interposed Lamb Ral, with decision, "we are about to go down into the valley. If you see any man attacking Mr. Jacobs, knock him down. If you cannot do that, shoot him under the arm. At any rate dispose of him. I am not Wiggins, but I predict a storm."

CHAPTER XIII.

After tiffin we went down into the valley to meet the emissary of a Certain Mighty Person and Number One. The emissary advanced with a scroll so illegible that Jacobs bent over it in despair. Taking advantage of his absorption, the villain put his hand upon my friend's shoulder. I sprang upon him like a bull-dog.

Meanwhile Lamb Ral created a pleasant diversion by drawing down from the sky a blood-curdling fog, heavier than the after-dinner speech of an alderman, more dense than the public taste, more paralyzing than the philosophy of the last popular novel. Dread and cottony, like a curtain, descended the awful cloud into the uplifted arms of the sleight-of-hand man, until I could not see an inch before my nose. Nevertheless I was able to observe that he had stretched himself, probably by an arrangement of crossed levers, to an incalculable height, and I distinctly observed him wink with one eye as I kneaded my adversary.

As I had just snapped the arm of the emissary like a pipe-stem and the rest had each killed somebody, the mist was opportune and our party skulked back to camp, where we all drank a good deal of tiffin. The result of our imbibing was that Jacobs clapped Number One on the shoulder.

"You're a bully good fellow," he observed, thickly. "Git!"

Lamb Ral and Number One disappeared in a red light, with plaintive music from the orchestra.

CHAPTER XIV.

We returned home.

"Miss Eastinhoe is dead!" I said to Mr. Jacobs.

"It is really better," remarked Lamb Ral, who chanced to be astrally present, being also in Ireland with Number One at the same moment. "There was absolutely no other way of concluding the story. She wouldn't be a fourth wife; besides, she was so shadowy a personage that nobody cared anything about her."

"No," said Mr. Jacobs. "I had wholly forgotten that."

"You had better go and be a nun," Lamb Ral continued, reclining upon a tiffin. "Trade is dull, and your last trick in glass emeralds has been discovered."

"On the whole I think I will," replied Jacobs. "Briggs, I have given my fortune to Miss Eastinhoe's brother, who rescued me from the gutter. To you I give this diamond. I know you too well to trust you with anything else. Nay," he added, seeing my inquiring look, "do not ask its price or try it with a file until I am gone."

"You won't come and be a nun yourself, Mr. Briggs?" Lamb Ral inquired, with some apprehension.

"Thanks, no," I answered, drawing my tiffin over my shoulders, "I'll write the thing up."

Mr. Jacobs

"Thank you, noble friend," Jacobs said, grasping my hand with emotion. "You have been the instructor and the genius of my love. I go to be a nun. Be yourself what you have made me."

One last, loving look,—one more pressure of the reluctant fingers, and those two went out, hand in hand, under the clear stars, and I saw them no more.

POSTSCRIPT.

I afterwards ascertained that the fortune left to Mr. Eastinhoe consisted chiefly of the three discarded wives of Mr. Jacobs.

"I had no means of supporting them," Mr. Eastinhoe remarked, gravely,—he was from Bombay, and Bombay men never smile,—"so I was forced to have them served for tiffin. What will you take?"

"A peg of tiffin," I replied, with a pensive sigh.

FINIS.

Mr. Jacobs

Copyright © 2023 Esprios Digital Publishing. All Rights Reserved.